WRITE SOURCE

SkillsBook

S0-AQL-200

GREAT SOURCE.

HOUGHTON MIFFLIN HARCOURT

About the *SkillsBook* . . .

The *Write Source SkillsBook* is a place to learn and to write. There are three sections in the *SkillsBook*. The first section focuses on skills and rules to help children grow as writers. The second section is a place to write—everything from journal entries to stories. The final section serves as a personal dictionary, a reference tool to use throughout the year.

Next Step

Many exercises end with a **Next Step** activity. It provides an opportunity for students to apply what they have learned to their own writing.

Copyright © by Houghton Mifflin Harcourt Publishing Company

Printed in the U.S.A.

ISBN   978-0-547-48431-0

19 0928 20

4500818047   A B C D E F G

We hope you will have fun writing!

This *SkillsBook* belongs to

Contents

A B C D E F G H I J K L M N O P Q R S T U V W X Y Z

Guided Writing Skills

Sentences

Punctuation

Grammar

Parts of Speech

Name: _____

Writing Sentences

When you write a sentence, you follow three important rules.

Rule 1 Start each sentence with a capital letter.

Rule 2 Leave space between your words.

Rule 3 End each sentence with an end mark.

The girl likes little cats.

Capital Letter   Space Between Words   End Mark

 A Trace these sentences. See how they follow the three sentence rules.

1. Jake likes dogs.

2. He likes puppies.

3. Juan likes jokes.

Write Source page 53

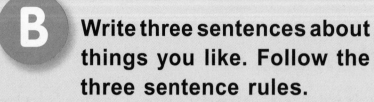
B Write three sentences about things you like. Follow the three sentence rules.

Sample:

I like rabbits.

1. I like

2. I like

3. I like

 **Next Step**

Draw a picture about one of your sentences.

Name: _____

Complete Thoughts

A **sentence** is a group of words that tells a complete thought.

This is a sentence.

> ## The bee sees a flower.

This is **not** a sentence.

> ## The buzzing bee.

 A **Circle the two complete sentences.**

1. The bee likes orange flowers.

2. The orange flowers.

3. Bees make honey.

4. Need the flowers.

B Finish each sentence with a word from the box below.

honey   sweet   like

1. The _____ is good.

2. It tastes _____.

3. I _____ to put honey on my toast.

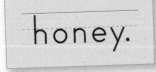

Next Step

Make a complete sentence. Write the words below in the correct order.

honey.   Bears   eat

_____

Name: _____

The Naming Part

Every sentence has a **naming part**. It tells *who* or *what* the sentence is about.

> Max climbs the jungle gym.

This naming part tells **who** climbs.

> The jungle gym is new.

This naming part tells **what** is new.

 A Read each sentence below. Color the ☺ if the underlined part is the naming part of the sentence.

1. <u>My jump rope</u> is long.

2. Mary <u>plays with me</u>.

3. <u>The boys</u> play, too.

Write Source pages 48–49

B Underline the naming part in each sentence.

1. My brother climbs the ladder.

2. Melissa swings high.

3. We play tag after school.

4. Our teacher blows her whistle.

 **Next Step**

Write a sentence about recess. Underline the naming part of your sentence. Share your sentence with a friend.

Name: _____

The Telling Part

Every sentence has a **telling part**. It tells something about the naming part.

> The family goes to the lake.

This telling part tells what the family is doing.

A Look at each picture. Draw a line from the naming part to the telling part to finish each sentence.

Naming Part   **Telling Part**

1.  A big fish   hop and hop.

2.  The duck   jumps.

3.  Rabbits   quacks.

B Circle the telling part in each sentence.

1. Grandma sits on the beach.

2. The children jump in the water.

3. Dad rows a boat.

4. Mom catches a fish.

Next Step

Write about a time you had fun outside. Finish the sentence below with your own telling part. Share your sentence with a friend.

One day, I

Name: _____

Sentence Parts

Every complete sentence has a naming part and a telling part.

Naming Part + Telling Part = Sentence

$$\boxed{\text{Meg}} + \boxed{\text{jumps}} = \boxed{\text{Meg jumps.}}$$

A Make a complete sentence that tells about each picture. Draw a line from each naming part to the correct telling part.

Naming Part	Telling Part

1.  The bird   rings a bell.

2.  My sister   cooks dinner.

3.  Dad   sings.

Write Source pages 52–53

B Finish each sentence with your own naming or telling part.

1. _____ likes to dance.

2. I ride _____ .

3. _____ wears glasses.

4. The kitten _____ .

 **Next Step**   Write a sentence about yourself. Draw a picture to go with it.

_____

Name: _____

Telling Sentences

A **telling sentence** tells about something or someone. Every telling sentence begins with a capital letter and ends with a period.

I see fish.

Capital Letter   End Mark

A Add more pictures and words to this page. You may color your pictures.

bubbles

feet

fish

weeds

Write Source pages 54–55

B Look at the picture on page 15. Then finish each telling sentence below. Tell about things you see.

Sample:

I see fish.

1. I see _____

2. I see _____

3. I see _____

Next Step

Write one sentence about what you might hear at the lake.

_____

_____

Name: _____

Asking Sentences

An **asking sentence** asks a question. Every asking sentence begins with a capital letter and ends with a question mark.

Do you see the kitten?

Capital Letter   End Mark

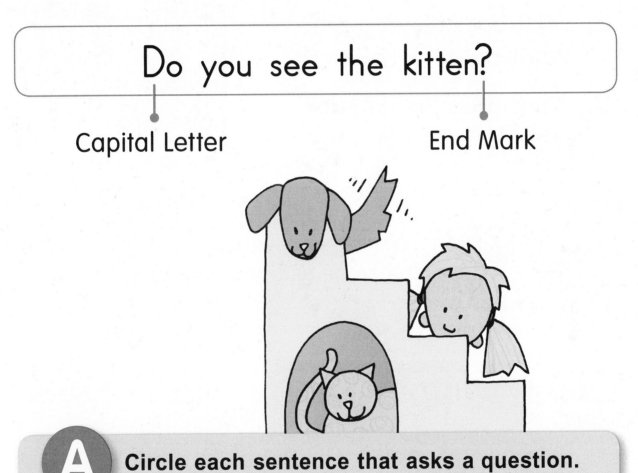

A Circle each sentence that asks a question.

1. Where is the kitten?

2. The kitten is under the steps.

3. Does the girl see the kitten?

B Circle the correct asking sentence in each set.

1. Where is the dog?
   Where is the dog.

2. what does the dog see?
   What does the dog see?

3. What does the dog do?
   What does the dog do

Next Step

Write these words in order to make an asking sentence.

 you   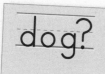 dog?   the   Do   see

Name: _____

Exclamatory Sentences

An **exclamatory sentence** shows strong feelings. Every exclamatory sentence begins with a capital letter and ends with an exclamation point.

Wow, it is raining hard!

Capital Letter   End Mark

A Add a period (.), a question mark (?), or an exclamation point (!) in the sentences below.

1. Should I get the umbrella ___

2. Yikes, I hear thunder ___

3. We should go inside ___

4. Quick, call the dog ___

Write Source pages 54–55

B Finish each sentence with a word from the box below.

> fast   Tory   rainbow

1. Come here, _____ !

2. Tory, run _____ !

3. Look, there's a _____ !

Next Step

Write an exclamatory sentence.
Tell about a time you were excited.

_____

_____

Name: _____

Sentence Review

A **telling sentence** tells about something or someone. It ends with a period.

> ## Grandma made soup.

An **asking sentence** asks a question. It ends with a question mark.

> ## Was the soup good?

An **exclamatory sentence** shows strong feelings. It ends with an exclamation point.

> ## Yes, it was delicious!

 A Add a period (.), a question mark (?), or an exclamation point (!) in the sentences below.

1. Do you like pizza ____

2. I love pizza ____

3. I like mine with sausage ____

Write Source pages 54–55

B Underline the correct sentence in each set.

1. My dad is in a band.
   my dad is in a band.

2. does he play the drums?
   Does he play the drums?

3. No, he plays a tuba.
   no, he plays a tuba.

4. wow, the tuba is huge!
   Wow, the tuba is huge!

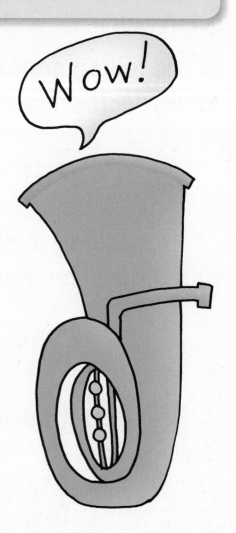

Next Step

Think of a question to ask one of your classmates. Write an asking sentence.

Name: _____

Periods

Use a **period** at the end of a telling sentence. A telling sentence tells a complete thought.

> I like to write stories.

End Mark

Use a period after an abbreviation.

| Mr. Kelly | Dr. Web | Mrs. Bell |

A Read both groups of words. Circle the group of words that makes a complete telling sentence.

1. At school.   I write at school.

2. I read my books.   My books.

3. I can paint.   Can paint.

4. And I play.   Bill and I play.

Write Source page 270

B Each sentence below is missing one period. Add a period after an abbreviation or at the end of the sentence.

1. Mr Mack is a firefighter.

2. He talked to our class about fire safety

3. We listened

4. Mrs Jones thanked him.

Check your smoke detectors.

Next Step Finish these two telling sentences with your own words. Use a period at the end of each sentence.

I saw _____

I am going _____

Name: _____

End Marks

Put a **question mark** after a sentence that asks a question.

> Did you see the big red rose?

Put an **exclamation point** after an exciting word or an exclamatory sentence.

> Ouch! It has a thorn!

 A **Read each sentence. Circle the correct end mark.**

1. Wow . ? !

2. Who will get these flowers . ? !

3. Surprise . ? !

4. Are the flowers for Grandmother . ? !

5. She smiled at me . ? !

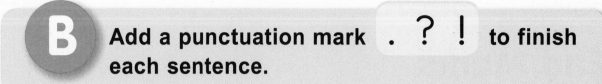

B Add a punctuation mark . ? ! to finish each sentence.

1. I am huge ___

I live in the ocean ___

What am I ___

_____

- - - - - - - - - - - -

_____

2. I have strong teeth ___

I build with wood ___

What am I ___

_____

- - - - - - - - - - - -

_____

3. I am a bird ___

I love the snow ___

What am I ___

_____

- - - - - - - - - - - -

_____

4. I have eight legs ___

I can spin webs ___

What am I ___

_____

- - - - - - - - - - - -

_____

C Answer the riddles above. Choose an answer from the box below.

spider   whale   penguin   beaver

Name: _____

Commas 1

Place a **comma** (**,**) in the date and after the greeting and closing in a letter.

Date	September 12, 2006
Greeting	Dear Tim,
Message	Bring your checkers to school. We can play during free time. It will be fun.
	Your friend,
Closing	Nick

 A **Add a comma in the correct place in these dates.**

1. January 20 2006

2. May 4 2005

3. July 15 2006

4. August 21 2007

B Add three commas in the letter below.

September 12 2006

Dear Nick
    The checkers are in my backpack. I also
brought my soccer ball. Maybe we can play outside.

        Your friend
        Tim

Next Step

Write a short letter to someone. Use commas correctly.

_____

Dear _____

_____

_____

        Your friend

        _____

Name: _____

Commas 2

Put **commas** between words in a series.

> I write with my pencils, crayons, and markers.

A Make a picture sentence. Then write words and commas.

I like [ ] , [ ] ,

_____ _____

_____ _____

and [ ] .

_____

_____ .

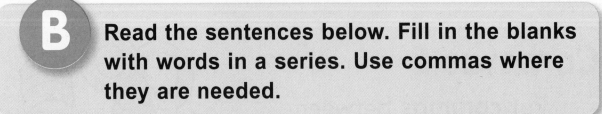
B Read the sentences below. Fill in the blanks with words in a series. Use commas where they are needed.

1. I like to eat _____ □ _____ □

and _____ .

2. _____ □ _____ □

and _____ live at the zoo.

 **Next Step** Write a sentence that names your three favorite colors. Use commas between the color words.

_____

_____

_____

Name: _____

Apostrophes

An **apostrophe** is used to make a contraction. A contraction is a new word that is made from two words. The apostrophe shows where letters are missing.

Two Words	Contraction
are not	aren't

 A Draw a line between the words and their contractions.

Two Words | **Contractions**

1. it is   he's

2. do not   I'm

3. I am   it's

4. he is   she's

5. she is   don't

Write Source pages 236–237 and 274

B **Write the contraction made from the words in ( ).**

1. _____ making a kite.
   (I am)

2. _____ red and yellow.
   (It is)

C **Write the two words for each contraction.**

1. I'm having fun. _____

2. It's a sunny day. _____

3. Look, he's riding a bike. _____

4. She's roller-skating. _____

Name: _____

Punctuation Review

Every sentence ends with an end mark.

- Telling sentences end with a period (.).
- Asking sentences end with a question mark (?).
- Exclamatory sentences end with an exclamation point (!).

 A **Add the correct end mark to each sentence.**

1. What is a pika ____

2. A pika is a cousin to the rabbit ____

3. Pikas live in the mountains ____

4. Wow, pikas are hard workers ____

B **Circle the correct contraction in each sentence.**

1. I (*didn't, isn't*) know about pikas.

2. (*I'm, Don't*) glad my teacher told me.

Write Source pages 236–237 and 270–274

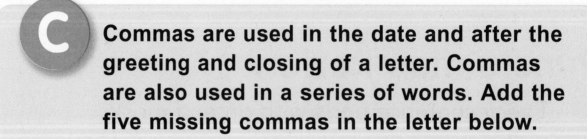
C Commas are used in the date and after the greeting and closing of a letter. Commas are also used in a series of words. Add the five missing commas in the letter below.

November 8 2012

Dear Grandpa

I read about pikas. Pikas are little animals. They know how to make hay. They hide from weasels coyotes and hawks. Have you ever seen a pika?

Love

Missy

Name: _____

Capital Letters 1

Use a **capital letter** at the beginning of each sentence. Also use a capital letter for the word **I**.

First Word of a Sentence

> Harbor seals eat fish.

The Word I

> May I eat some fish, too?

 A **Put three lines (☰) under the letter that should be a capital letter in each sentence below.**

1. seagulls eat fish.

2. Once, i saw a seagull flying.

3. it dove into the water.

4. Then i saw the gull fly away with a fish.

Write Source page 275

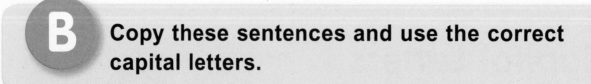

B **Copy these sentences and use the correct capital letters.**

1. My dad and i see a pelican.

_____

- -

_____

_____

- -

_____

2. the pelican has a pouch.

_____

- -

_____

_____

- -

_____

Next Step **Write a sentence about a bird that you have seen.**

_____

- -

_____

_____

- -

_____

Name: _____

Capital Letters 2

Capital letters are used at the beginning of special names and in name titles.

For Special Names

Rosa Parks Ohio Texas

For Name Titles

Mrs. Cooper Mr. Ford

 A Circle the word or title in each sentence that should begin with a capital letter.

1. Mr. lee lives in Ohio.

2. My teacher is ms. Miller.

3. I live in new York.

4. Mrs. smith is my neighbor.

Write Source page 276

B Draw a picture of yourself with a friend.
Then write your names below your pictures.

 **Next Step**   Look at a map of the United States. Write the name of one state that you would like to visit.

Name: _____

Capital Letters 3

Use **capital letters** when you write the days of the week, months of the year, and special holidays.

Days of the Week

| Sunday   Friday |

Months of the Year

| January   May |

Holidays

| Arbor Day   Thanksgiving |

 A Circle the word in each sentence that should begin with a capital letter. Then write the word correctly.

1. Library day is friday.

_____

_____

2. The first month of the year is january.

_____

_____

Write Source pages 276–277

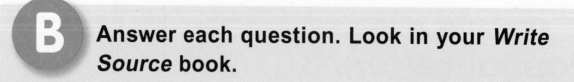
B **Answer each question. Look in your _Write Source_ book.**

1. What day of the week is it today? (Page 258)

_____

- -

_____

2. Which month are we in? (Page 259)

_____

- -

_____

3. What is your favorite holiday? (Page 276)

_____

- -

_____

 **Next Step**

Write one sentence about a month. Use the name of the month in your sentence.

_____

- -

_____

Name: _____

Capital-Letter Review

A Special names of people, places, and things begin with capital letters. Write the name of someone you know and the name of a special place.

Person

_____

- - - - - - - - - - - - - - - -

_____

Place

_____

- - - - - - - - - - - - - - - -

_____

B Every sentence begins with a capital letter. The word *I* always uses a capital letter. Write each word that needs a capital letter in these sentences.

1. my aunt lives in New York.

_____

- - - - - - - - - - - - - - - - - - - -

_____

2. Tomorrow, i will visit her.

_____

- - - - - - - - - - - - - - - - - - - -

_____

C Name titles begin with a capital letter. Write each name title correctly.

1. mrs. Nora

_____

- - - - - - - - - - - - - - - -

_____

2. mr. Rios

_____

- - - - - - - - - - - - - - - -

_____

D Days of the week, months of the year, and names of holidays begin with capital letters. Write each underlined word correctly.

1. I love the month of <u>november</u>!

_____

- - - - - - - - - - - - - - - -

_____

2. A holiday happens on the last <u>thursday</u>.

_____

- - - - - - - - - - - - - - - -

_____

Name: _____

Plurals 1

Add an **-s** to make the plural of most nouns.
The word **plural** means more than one.

One		**More Than One**	
ant		ants	
snake		snakes	

A Write each noun so that it means more than one.

 1. bat _____

 **2.** bear _____

 3. duck _____

Write Source pages 223, 278, and 292

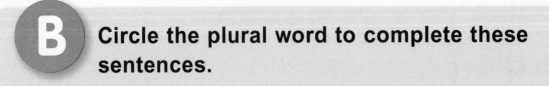
B Circle the plural word to complete these sentences.

1. Some (*zebra, zebras*) race.

2. Two (*bird, birds*) eat seeds.

3. Casey watches three (*hippo, hippos*).

4. A family of (*ape, apes*) lives in the zoo.

5. Tigers and lions are big (*cat, cats*).

 **Next Step** Write a sentence using the plural word for **horse**.

Name: _____

Plurals 2

Some nouns use different words to show more than one.

one child	three children

A Draw a line from the word that means one to the word that means more than one.

One   **More Than One**

1.   foot   teeth

2. man   women

3. mouse   feet

4. tooth   men

5.   woman   mice

Write Source page 278

> **B** Look at the word below each line. Fill in the blank with the correct plural word to finish each sentence.

1. Many _____ go to my school.
(children, child)

2. My cat chased two _____.
(mouse, mice)

3. Three _____ watched the game.
(men, man)

4. My friend lost two _____.
(tooth, teeth)

5. My _____ got wet in the puddle.
(foot, feet)

Name: _____

Plurals Review

A Look at the words below each line. Write the plural word to finish each sentence.

1. Students study many _____ and women.
(man, men)

2. _____ read about folk heroes.
(Children, Child)

3. Johnny Appleseed walked with bare _____.
(foot, feet)

4. He always carried apple _____.
(seeds, seed)

5. He planted apple _____ everywhere.
(tree, trees)

Write Source pages 223, 278, and 292

ABCDEFGHIJKLMNOPQRSTUVWXYZ

B Draw a line from the word that means one to the word that means more than one.

One   **More Than One**

 pail   books

book   shoes

shoe   pails

C Write the plural word in each blank.

1. Johnny had many _____ of seeds.
   (bag, bags)

2. He walked for _____ .
   (miles, mile)

3. Johnny made many _____ .
   (friend, friends)

© Houghton Mifflin Harcourt Publishing Company

Name: _____

ABC Order 1

ABC order means words are in the same order as the letters in the alphabet. Look at the first letter of each word.

apple	banana	carrot

A Read the words in the box below. Write the words in ABC order.

butterfly	cat	ape	duck

1. _____

2. _____

3. _____

4. _____

Write Source page 279

B Read each question. Answer it with a word from the list below. Write the letters of the correct word in the blue boxes.

butterfly   cat   ape   duck

1. Which animal can swing in trees?

2. Which word names an insect?

3. Which animal purrs?

4. What animal likes to swim?

Name: _____

ABC Order 2

A Read the words in the box below. Write the words in ABC order.

house   goat   eagle   fish

1. _____

2. _____

3. _____

4. _____

B Use a word from the box below to finish each sentence.

house   goat   eagle   fish

1. The _____ lays eggs.

2. A _____ has fins.

3. A _____ has four legs.

4. Our dog has his own _____ .

 **Next Step**   List four more words that start with the letter **h**.

_____

_____

_____

Name: _____

ABC Order 3

A Read the words in the box below. Write the words in ABC order.

kite   igloo   jacket   ladybug

1. _____

2. _____

3. _____

4. _____

Write Source pages 280–281

B Find a word from the list that fits each set of boxes. Write the words.

kite   igloo   jacket   ladybug

1.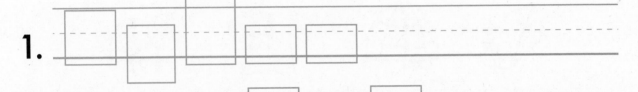

2.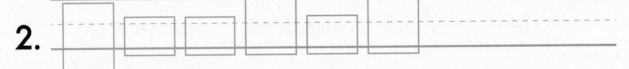

3.

4.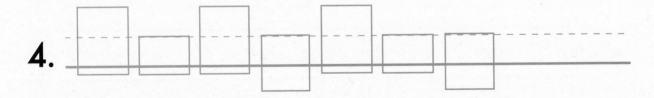

 **Next Step**   Imagine you are a ladybug. Write one sentence telling what you see or do.

Name: _____

ABC Order 4

A Read the words in the box below. Write the words in ABC order.

penguin   moose   octopus   nest

1. _____

2. _____

3. _____

4. _____

B Write the word from the box below that tells about each picture.

penguin   moose   octopus   nest

1. _____

2. _____

3. _____

4. _____

Next Step Write a sentence about an animal that builds a nest.

_____

_____

_____

Name: _____

ABC Order 5

A Read the words in the box below. Write the words in ABC order.

rabbit   socks   quilt   turtle

1. _____

2. _____

3. _____

4. _____

B **Write the words from the box on the lines below. Fill in the missing letters.**

| rabbit   socks   quilt   turtle |

1. __ u __ l __

2. __ a __ b __ t

3. __ o __ k s

4. __ __ r __ l e

 **Next Step**

Write a sentence using one of the four words above.

_____

- -

_____

- -

_____

Name: _____

ABC Order 6

A Read the words in the box below. Write the words in ABC order.

zebra	umbrella	wagon
vase	yarn	X-ray

1._____   4._____

2._____   5._____

3._____   6._____

B Read the words in the box below. Write the word that answers each riddle.

zebra	umbrella	wagon
vase	yarn	X-ray

1. I keep you dry when it rains.

___ ___ ___ ___ ___ ___ ___ ___

2. I hold flowers.

___ ___ ___ ___

3. I have wheels.

___ ___ ___ ___ ___

4. I am used by doctors.

___-___ ___ ___

5. I am used to make a pair of mittens.

___ ___ ___ ___

6. I am a black and white animal.

___ ___ ___ ___ ___

Name: _____

Using the Right Word 1

Homophones

 **A** **Write the correct word for each sentence.**

ate	eight

_____

1. Jack _____ a big apple.

_____

2. Write the number _____ .

B **Write the correct word for each sentence.**

blew	blue

_____

1. The wind _____ the man's hat off.

_____

2. I want the _____ crayon.

C **Write the correct word for each sentence.**

> buy   by

1. Did you walk _____ the park?

2. Mother wants to _____ some milk.

D **Write the correct word for each sentence.**

> dear   deer

1. We saw _____ in the woods.

2. My _____ aunt will visit us today.

Name: _____

Using the Right Word 2

A Write the correct word for each sentence.

| for   four |

1. Sam had soup _____ lunch.

2. I have _____ books about dinosaurs.

B Write the correct word for each sentence.

| read   red |

1. Jill is wearing a _____ ribbon today.

2. She has _____ many books.

C Write the correct word for each sentence.

hear	here

1. I can _____ a bird.

2. It is over _____ .

D Write the correct word for each sentence.

know	no

1. Do you _____ what day it is?

2. Oh _____ ! I lost my paper.

Name: _____

Using the Right Word 3

A Write the correct word for each sentence.

one	won

1. May I borrow _____ crayon?

2. Alex _____ a race.

B Write the correct word for each sentence.

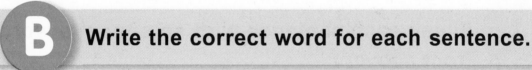

road	rode

1. Our new mailbox is by the _____ .

2. I _____ on the city bus.

Write Source pages 285–286

Using an Opposite Word

Antonyms are two words with opposite meanings.

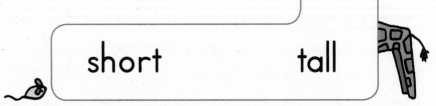

short   tall

 A **Draw a line from the word on the left to its opposite.**

1. happy   off

2. on   sad

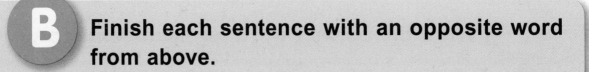 **B** **Finish each sentence with an opposite word from above.**

1. One puppy looked <u>happy</u>.

The other puppy looked _____.

2. Did you turn the light <u>on</u>?

Please turn it _____.

Name: _____

Nouns

A **noun** is a word that names a person, place, or thing.

Person	Place	Thing
farmer	park	bicycle

A Circle what each noun names.

1. doctor   person   place   thing

2. bone   person   place   thing

3. playground   person   place   thing

B Read each sentence. Draw a line under each noun. The number in ( ) tells how many nouns are in each sentence.

1. Tom goes to the city. (2)

2. Many people walk by. (1)

3. Cars honk their horns. (2)

Write Source pages 220–221 and 291

ABCDEFGHIJKLMNOPQRSTUVWXYZ

C Write each noun in the correct list under **Person**, **Place**, or **Thing**.

|  plane |  Mr. Vu |  hen |
|  farm |  baby |  garden |

Person

Place

Thing

Next Step Write a sentence about recess. Underline each noun.

Name: _____

Common and Proper Nouns

A **common noun** names any person, place, or thing. A **proper noun** names a special person, place, or thing. A proper noun always begins with a capital letter.

Common Nouns	Proper Nouns
boy	Henry
city	Portland

 A Draw a circle around the proper noun for each picture.

1. 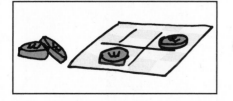 woman   Mrs. Wolf

2. Shell Beach   beach

3. Checkeroo   game

     Write Source pages 222 and 291

B **Draw a picture of your family. Write the name of each person next to his or her picture.**

Name: _____

Singular and Plural Nouns

Nouns are singular or plural. A **singular noun** names one person, place, or thing. A **plural noun** names more than one person, place, or thing. A plural noun usually end with an **–s**.

Singular   **Plural**

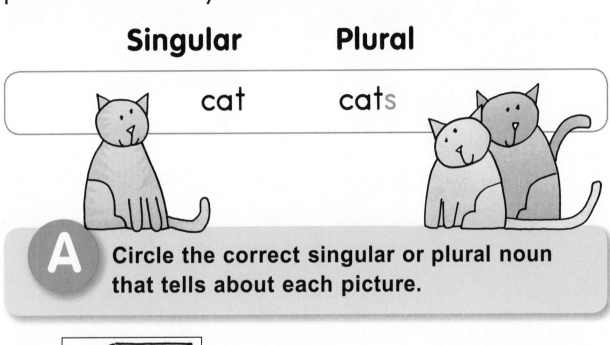

cat   cats

A Circle the correct singular or plural noun that tells about each picture.

1. book   books

2. girl   girls

3. cup   cups

4. hat   hats

Write Source pages 223 and 292

A B C D E F G H I J K L M N O P Q R S T U V W X Y Z

B Write the plural of each noun on the lines below.

1. train

_____

2. boat

_____

3. truck

_____

4. ship

_____

 **Next Step**

Write a sentence using one of the plural nouns above.

_____

_____

Name: _____

Pronouns

A **pronoun** is a word that takes the place of a noun.

Nouns	**Pronouns**
Neil eats grapes.	He eats grapes.
Tory likes pears.	She likes pears.
Neil and Tory like fruit.	They like fruit.

 A **Draw a line from each word or words to the pronoun that can take its place.**

1. Mother and Father   it

2. pencil   he

3. Bob and I   they

4. Paulo   we

Write Source pages 224–227 and 293

B Read each sentence below. Write the pronoun that can take the place of each underlined noun.

He   She   They

1. Adam runs fast.

_____

- - - - - - - - - - -

_____

2. Rene jumps high.

_____

- - - - - - - - - - -

_____

3. The boys and girls play outside.

_____

- - - - - - - - - - -

_____

 **Next Step**

Write a sentence. Use the pronoun **we**.

_____

- -

_____

_____

- -

_____

Name: _____

Verbs

Some **verbs** show action.

April smiles.
She waves at me.

A Draw a line from the verb to the picture that shows the correct action.

1. jump

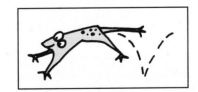

2. run

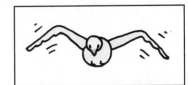

3. swim

4. fly

Write Source pages 229 and 294

B Circle the action verb in each sentence below.

1. Max rides his bike.

2. He wears a helmet.

3. Max sees Jill.

4. Jill runs to Max.

5. They play together.

C Write a verb from the box to finish each sentence below.

| fly | race | spin |

1. My bike tires _____ .

2. I _____ down the sidewalk.

3. Planes _____ high.

Name: _____

Tenses of Action Verbs

A **present-tense verb** tells what is happening now. A **past-tense verb** tells what has already happened. Most past tense verbs end with **–ed**.

Present Tense

> Jane and Papa walk to the barn.

Past Tense

> Jane and Papa walked to the barn.

 A   **Read each sentence. Circle the action verb that tells what is happening now.**

1. Papa *(opens, opened)* a gate.

2. He *(looks, looked)* at a goat.

3. The goat *(lifts, lifted)* its head.

4. Then Jane *(hands, handed)* the goat some corn.

Write Source pages 230–231 and 295

A B C D E F G H I J K L M N O P Q R S T U V W X Y Z

B **Read each sentence. Write the action verb that tells what has already happened.**

1. Yesterday, Jane _____ with Papa.
   (works, worked)

2. Papa _____ the goat's stall.
   (cleaned, cleans)

3. Jane _____ new hay for the goat.
   (stacked, stacks)

4. Papa _____ her for helping.
   (thanks, thanked)

 Next Step **Write a sentence using a past-tense verb.**

_____

_____

_____

Name: _____

Linking Verbs 1

A **linking verb** helps complete a thought.

> Joel is tall.
>
> I am his cousin.

Common Linking Verbs

> am   is   are   was   were

 A Circle the linking verb in each sentence.

1. Saturday is a busy time.

2. I am sleepy.

3. The barking dogs are noisy.

4. The water is cold.

5. I am a soccer player.

B   Circle the correct linking verb in each sentence.

am	is	are

1. Heath *(am, is)* my neighbor.

2. We *(am, are)* friends.

3. I *(am, are)* happy he moved next door.

C   Write the correct linking verb to finish each sentence.

1. Today _____ a special day for my family.
     (am, is)

2. We _____ excited about Grandma's visit.
     (am, are)

3. I _____ her only grandson.
     (am, is)

Name: _____

Linking Verbs 2

A linking verb helps complete a thought.

> I was hungry.
> We were friends.

 A Circle the correct verb in each sentence.

was	were

1. Cody and Brian *(was, were)* excited yesterday.

2. Cody *(was, were)* helpful last night.

3. Brian *(was, were)* late this morning.

B Draw a line from each naming part to the telling part with the correct linking verb.

1. Nelly   were absent.

2. Niki and Nelly   was sick last week.

Write Source pages 232–233 and 296

Circle the correct linking verb to finish each sentence.

1. The table *(was, were)* messy.

2. The dishes *(was, were)* dirty.

3. My cousin and I *(was, were)* helpful.

4. My dad *(was, were)* proud of us.

D Write a naming part for each telling part in the sentences below.

1. _____ was my teacher last year.

2. _____ and _____ were at home.

3. _____ was fun.

4. _____ and _____ were delicious.

Name: _____

Adjectives

An **adjective** is a word that tells something about a noun. Adjectives can tell **what kind** or **how many**.

A Circle the adjective that tells something about the underlined noun in each sentence.

1. Here comes a long <u>train</u>.

2. The train has two <u>engineers</u>.

3. The red <u>caboose</u> is last.

B Write the correct adjective from the box to finish each sentence.

loud   seven

1. I heard a _____ train engine.

2. It pulled _____ boxcars.

Write Source pages 238–239 and 297

Adjectives That Compare

Some adjectives **compare** people, places, or things. If an adjective compares two people, places, or things, add **–er**.

> A whale is longer than a goldfish.

If an adjective compares more than two people, places, or things, add **–est**.

> The whale is the longest mammal alive.

A Write the correct adjective in each sentence.

1. A giraffe is _____ than a fox.

    (taller, tallest)

2. A mouse is _____ than a fox.

    (smaller, smallest)

3. The giraffe is the_____ of the three.

    (larger, largest)

Name: _____

Parts of Speech Review

A A noun is a word that names a person, place, or thing. Write the noun from each sentence below.

1. Come to the kitchen.

_____

- - - - - - - - - - - - - - -

_____

2. Dad cooks for us.

_____

- - - - - - - - - - - - - - -

_____

3. We eat tacos.

_____

- - - - - - - - - - - - - - -

_____

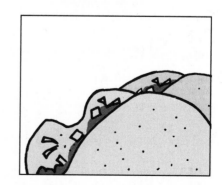

Write Source pages 220–235 and 291–296

B A pronoun takes the place of a noun. Circle the correct pronoun for each underlined noun or nouns.

1. <u>Christine</u> makes her bed.

    It   They   She

2. <u>Joshua and Christine</u> are good helpers.

    It   They   I

C Verbs show action or help complete a thought. Write the correct verb to finish each sentence.

1. Aunt Jo_____ us.

    (surprises, surprise)

2. She _____ us new books.

    (brings, bring)

3. We _____ very happy.

    (is, are)

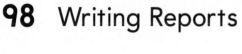

Writing Practice

Writing in Journals

Writers use journals every day. They write about what they see and do. They share their thoughts. Sometimes they even draw pictures.

Think about what happened today. Then write about it.

_____

- - - - - - - - - - - - - - - - - - -

_____

Date

_____

- - - - - - - - - - - - - - - - - - -

_____

- - - - - - - - - - - - - - - - - - -

_____

- - - - - - - - - - - - - - - - - - -

_____

- - - - - - - - - - - - - - - - - - -

_____

Name: _____

Writing Lists

One way to gather ideas about a topic is to make a list.

 Think of an interesting topic. Write a list of ideas you know about it.

A List About _____

(your topic)

_____

- -

_____

_____

- -

_____

_____

- -

_____

_____

- -

_____

Name: _____

Writing Friendly Notes

When you want to say thank you or hello, you can write a note.

 Write a friendly note to someone you know.

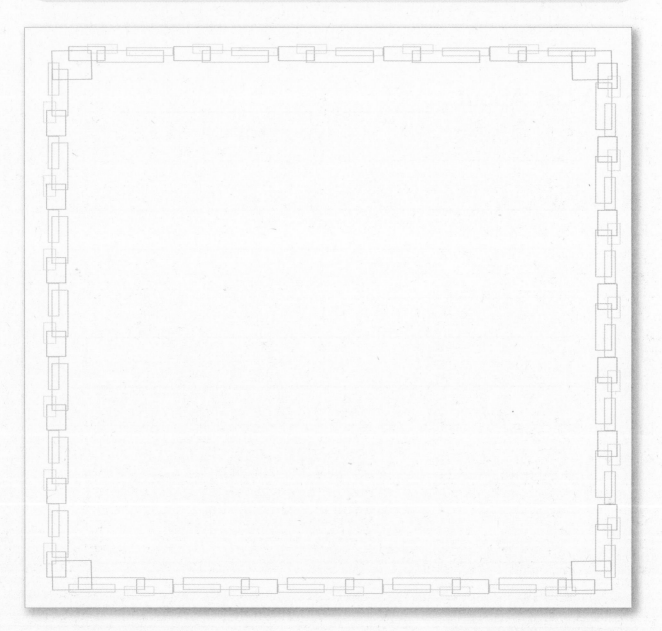

Name: _____

Writing Friendly Letters

You can write a **friendly letter** to someone near or faraway.

Date _____

Greeting _____

Message _____

Closing _____

Your name _____

Name: _____

Writing Descriptions

You can use your senses when you write about people, places, and things.

 Draw or attach a picture of a person, place, or thing.

Use your sensory chart to write about your picture.

Topic:_____

see	
hear	
smell	
taste	
touch	

Name: _____

Writing Narratives

You can write about things you have seen or done. Be sure to tell how you felt.

 Plan your story about a happy time.

1. Where were you?	**2.** Who was with you?
3. What happened?	**4.** What else happened?

Write your story about a happy time.

A Happy Time

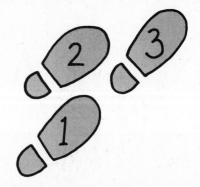
Name: _____

Writing How-To's

You can write about how to do something. Use an order chart to write the steps in order.

 Choose something you know how to do. Draw pictures of the steps you follow when you do it.

Topic: _____

Step 1	
Step 2	
Step 3	
Step 4	

Now write about each step. (Use your pictures on page 96 to help you.)

1. _____

2. _____

3. _____

4. _____

A B C D E F G H I J K L M N O P Q R S T U V W X Y Z

Name: _____

Writing Reports

When you write a report, you share facts with your reader. First, you pick a topic and gather details.

  Fill in a details sheet for your topic.

Details Sheet

1. My animal is the _____
   _____ .

2. Where does the animal live?
   _____
   _____

3. What does the animal look like?
   _____
   _____

4. How big or small is the animal?
   _____
   _____

5. What does the animal eat?
   _____
   _____

My Animal Report

A B C D E F G H I J K L M N O P Q R S T U V W X Y Z

My Own
Word Dictionary

My Words and Pictures

about

all

am

and

are

ask

at

away

Acorns
5¢

Aa Bb Cc Dd Ee Ff Gg Hh Ii Jj Kk Ll Mm

Nn Oo Pp Qq Rr Ss Tt Uu Vv Ww Xx Yy Zz

My Words and Pictures

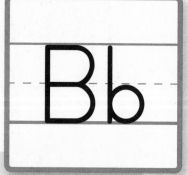

be

big

black

blue

brown

bug

but

by

ball

bus

Aa **Bb** Cc Dd Ee Ff Gg Hh Ii Jj Kk Ll Mm

Nn Oo Pp Qq Rr Ss Tt Uu Vv Ww Xx Yy Zz

My Words and Pictures

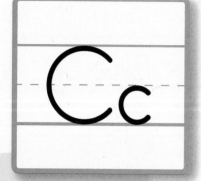

Cc

call

came

can

can't

circle

cold

color

come

Aa Bb **Cc** Dd Ee Ff Gg Hh Ii Jj Kk Ll Mm

Nn Oo Pp Qq Rr Ss Tt Uu Vv Ww Xx Yy Zz

A B C D E F G H I J K L M N O P Q R S T U V W X Y Z

My Words and Pictures

day

did

do

does

dog

don't

down

draw

Aa Bb Cc Dd Ee Ff Gg Hh Ii Jj Kk Ll Mm

N n O o P p Q q R r S s T t U u V v W w X x Y y Z z

My Words and Pictures

E e

each

ear

easy

eat

eight

end

every

eye

Aa Bb Cc Dd **Ee** Ff Gg Hh Ii Jj Kk Ll Mm

Nn Oo Pp Qq Rr Ss Tt Uu Vv Ww Xx Yy Zz

A B C D E F G H I J K L M N O P Q R S T U V W X Y Z

My Words and Pictures

Ff

feet

find

first

five

for

four

Friday

from

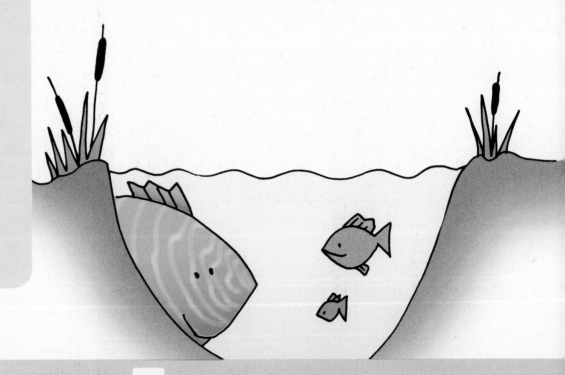

Aa Bb Cc Dd Ee **Ff** Gg Hh Ii Jj Kk Ll Mm

Nn Oo Pp Qq Rr Ss Tt Uu Vv Ww Xx Yy Zz

My Words and Pictures

Gg

get

give

go

goes

good

gray

green

grow

Aa Bb Cc Dd Ee Ff **Gg** Hh Ii Jj Kk Ll Mm

Nn Oo Pp Qq Rr Ss Tt Uu Vv Ww Xx Yy Zz

My Words and Pictures

Hh

had

has

have

he

help

here

home

how

Aa Bb Cc Dd Ee Ff Gg Hh Ii Jj Kk Ll Mm

Nn Oo Pp Qq Rr Ss Tt Uu Vv Ww Xx Yy Zz

My Words and Pictures

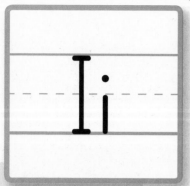

I

idea

if

I'm

in

into

is

it

Aa Bb Cc Dd Ee Ff Gg Hh **Ii** Jj Kk Ll Mm

N n O o P p Q q R r S s T t U u V v W w X x Y y Z z

My Words and Pictures

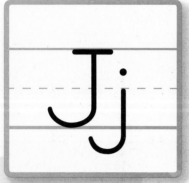

jar

jelly

job

joke

jump

just

Aa Bb Cc Dd Ee Ff Gg Hh Ii **Jj** Kk Ll Mm

Nn Oo Pp Qq Rr Ss Tt Uu Vv Ww Xx Yy Zz

My Words and Pictures

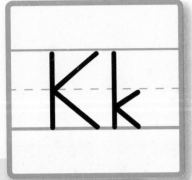

Kk

keep

kind

king

kitten

knee

knew

knot

know

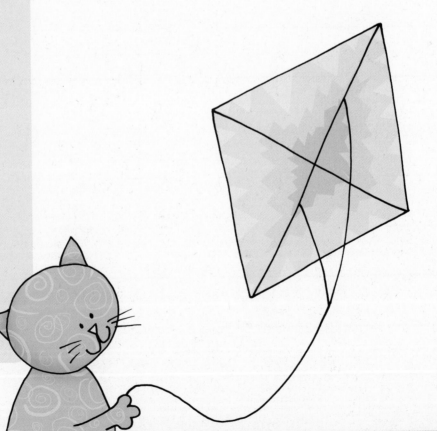

Aa Bb Cc Dd Ee Ff Gg Hh Ii Jj Kk Ll Mm

Nn Oo Pp Qq Rr Ss Tt Uu Vv Ww Xx Yy Zz

My Words and Pictures

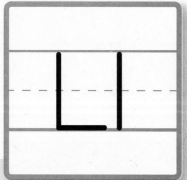

last

left

let

like

little

live

long

look

Aa Bb Cc Dd Ee Ff Gg Hh Ii Jj Kk **Ll** Mm

Nn Oo Pp Qq Rr Ss Tt Uu Vv Ww Xx Yy Zz

My Words and Pictures

made

make

many

me

Monday

most

must

my

Aa Bb Cc Dd Ee Ff Gg Hh Ii Jj Kk Ll **Mm**

Nn Oo Pp Qq Rr Ss Tt Uu Vv Ww Xx Yy Zz

My Words and Pictures

name

new

next

nine

no

nose

not

now

Aa Bb Cc Dd Ee Ff Gg Hh Ii Jj Kk Ll Mm

Nn Oo Pp Qq Rr Ss Tt Uu Vv Ww Xx Yy Zz

My Words and Pictures

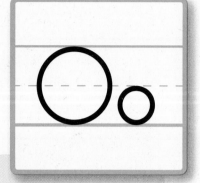

of

off

on

one

or

orange

our

out

Aa Bb Cc Dd Ee Ff Gg Hh Ii Jj Kk Ll Mm

Nn Oo Pp Qq Rr Ss Tt Uu Vv Ww Xx Yy Zz

My Words and Pictures

paper

people

play

please

pretty

pull

purple

put

Aa Bb Cc Dd Ee Ff Gg Hh Ii Jj Kk Ll Mm

N n O o P p Q q R r S s T t U u V v W w X x Y y Z z

My Words and Pictures

quack

question

quick

quiet

quit

quiz

Aa Bb Cc Dd Ee Ff Gg Hh Ii Jj Kk Ll Mm

My Words and Pictures

Rr

rain

ran

red

ride

right

ring

round

run

Aa Bb Cc Dd Ee Ff Gg Hh Ii Jj Kk Ll Mm

My Words and Pictures

Ss

said

Saturday

saw

say

seven

she

six

Sunday

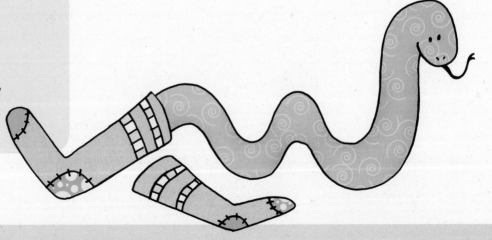

Aa Bb Cc Dd Ee Ff Gg Hh Ii Jj Kk Ll Mm

N n   O o   P p   Q q   R r   S s   T t   U u   V v   W w   X x   Y y   Z z

My Words and Pictures

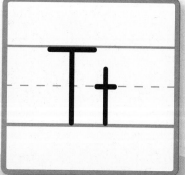

ten

the

they

this

three

Thursday

Tuesday

two

Aa Bb Cc Dd Ee Ff Gg Hh Ii Jj Kk Ll Mm

Nn Oo Pp Qq Rr Ss Tt Uu Vv Ww Xx Yy Zz

My Words and Pictures

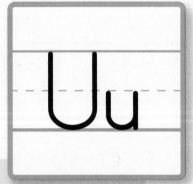

under

until

up

upon

us

use

Aa Bb Cc Dd Ee Ff Gg Hh Ii Jj Kk Ll Mm

Nn Oo Pp Qq Rr Ss Tt Uu Vv Ww Xx Yy Zz

My Words and Pictures

van

vegetable

very

vet

visit

voice

Aa Bb Cc Dd Ee Ff Gg Hh Ii Jj Kk Ll Mm

My Words and Pictures

want

was

we

Wednesday

were

what

white

who

Aa Bb Cc Dd Ee Ff Gg Hh Ii Jj Kk Ll Mm

Nn Oo Pp Qq Rr Ss Tt Uu Vv Ww Xx Yy Zz

My Words and Pictures

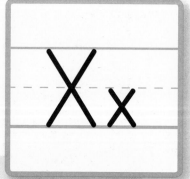

X-ray

fa<u>x</u>

fi<u>x</u>

mi<u>x</u>

si<u>x</u>

wa<u>x</u>

Aa Bb Cc Dd Ee Ff Gg Hh Ii Jj Kk Ll Mm

Nn Oo Pp Qq Rr Ss Tt Uu Vv Ww Xx Yy Zz

My Words and Pictures

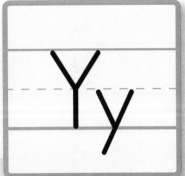

yawn

year

yellow

yes

you

your

Aa Bb Cc Dd Ee Ff Gg Hh Ii Jj Kk Ll Mm

Nn Oo Pp Qq Rr Ss Tt Uu Vv Ww Xx Yy Zz

My Words and Pictures

Zz

zebra

zero

zigzag

zip

zoo

zoom

Zoo

Aa Bb Cc Dd Ee Ff Gg Hh Ii Jj Kk Ll Mm

Write more words and draw more pictures.

Write more words and draw more pictures.

ABC Poem

Read this "ABC Poem" just for fun. Add some of your own drawings if you wish.

Alligator sits,
Butterfly flits.

Girl named Mary,
Hat for Harry.

Cup of tea,
Duck at sea.

Igloo white,
Jacket bright.

to cook,
a brook.

Kite in the sky,
Ladybug shy.

Mouse **near a hole,**
Nest **like a bowl.**

Umbrella **for showers,**
Vase **full of flowers.**

Octopus **below,**
Penguin **in the snow.**

Wagon **to pull,**
Box **full of wool.**

Quilt **for a bed,**
Rocket **that's red.**

Yarn **soft and blue,**
Zipper-dee-do!

Socks **for running,**
Turtle **goes sunning.**

We hope you had fun writing in your *SkillsBook*. Keep writing!

—Your Book Friends